what the Bible
has to say about:
children

ISBN 0-687-07522-X

Scripture quotations are taken from the HOLY BIBLE, NEW INTERNATIONAL VERSION ®. Copyright © 1973, 1978, 1984 International Bible Society.

Original edition published in English under the title What God Has to Say About: Children by John Hunt Publishing Ltd, New Alresford, Hants, UK.

This book was conceived, designed, and produced by

THE PALM PRESS

The Old Candlemakers, West Street
Lewes, East Sussex BN7 2NZ, UK

Creative Director: PETER BRIDGEWATER

Publisher: SOPHIE COLLINS

Editorial Director: STEVE LUCK

Designer: ANDREW MILNE

Project Editor: MANDY GREENFIELD

03 04 05 06 07 08 09 10 11 12 — 10 9 8 7 6 5 4 3 2 1

Manufactured in China

what the Bible has to say about:
children

Mark Water

DIMENSIONS
FOR LIVING
NASHVILLE

And he took

the children

in his arms,

put his hands

on them and

blessed them.

Mark 10: 16

Introduction The Police Department of Houston, Texas, issued the following document, entitled *Twelve Rules for Spoiling a Child*:

1 Begin at infancy to give the child everything he wants. In this way he will grow up to believe that the world owes him a living.

2 When he picks up bad words, laugh at him. This will make him think he's cute.

3 Never give him any spiritual training. Wait until he is 21 and then let him decide for himself.

4 Avoid the word "wrong." The child may develop a guilt complex.

5 Do everything for him so that he will be experienced in throwing all responsibility on other people.

6 Let him read any printed material he can get his hands on.

7 Quarrel frequently in the presence of your children.

8 Give a child all the spending money he wants.

9 Satisfy every craving for food, drink, and comfort.

10 Take his side against neighbors, teachers, and policemen.

11 When he gets into real trouble, apologize for him yourself.

12 Prepare for a life of grief.

God has given us certain principles to help us raise a family that we ignore at our peril.

Your wife will be like a fruitful vine

within your house;

your sons will be like olive shoots

around your table.

Psalm 128: 3

contents

Part 1
Babies

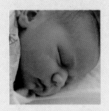

8

Introduction "Train a child in the way he should go, and when he is old he will not turn from it," says Proverbs 22: 6. If only it was that easy! But then, who ever said it would be easy to bring up a family, in any society, let alone in the 21st century?

One principle to hang on to, especially in the difficult early years of bringing up children, is God's unconditional love toward us. For example, in Jeremiah 31: 3 we read: "I have loved you with an everlasting love; I have drawn you with loving-kindness." God never ceases to love us, no matter how dreadful we are. In the same way, we don't stop loving our babies after endless sleepless nights, early mornings, and fractious days.

Here are five negatives to focus the aims of parents:

1 *If a child lives with criticism, he learns to condemn.*

2 *If a child lives with hostility, he learns to fight.*

3 *If a child lives with fear, he learns to be apprehensive.*

4 *If a child lives with pity, he learns to feel sorry for himself.*

5 *If a child lives with jealousy, he learns to feel guilty.*

Children are a gift

Sons are a heritage from the LORD, children a reward from him.   Psalm 127: 3

The Israelites saw children as a gift from the Lord. This influenced their whole outlook on raising children, educating children, loving children, and teaching their children about God's love.

11

A full quiver

Blessed is the man whose quiver is full of them [children].

Psalm 127: 5

In Old Testament days a large family was seen as a blessing from the Lord. But the Bible does not lay down how many children a particular family should have. There should be no pressure on couples even to start a family, let alone to have more children.

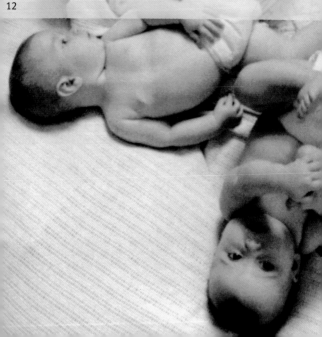

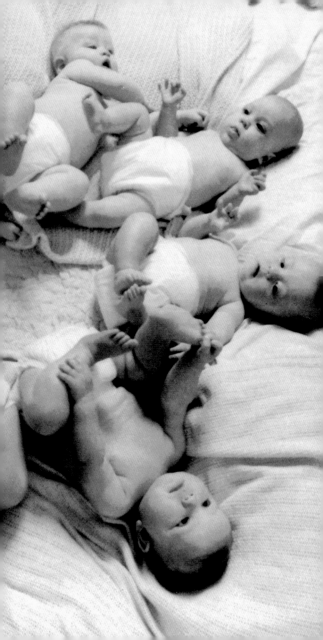

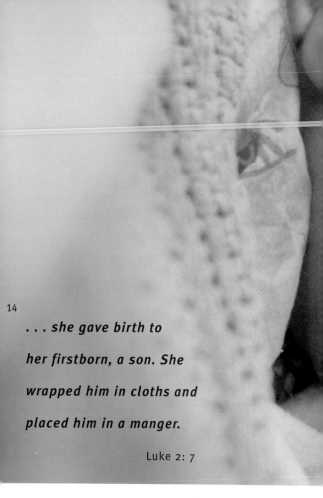

14

. . . she gave birth to her firstborn, a son. She wrapped him in cloths and placed him in a manger.

Luke 2: 7

Parents never forget the miracle of the birth of their first child. In the midst of the total disruption that this new life brings, and the years of constant attention ahead, the wonder of a new life will never be forgotten.

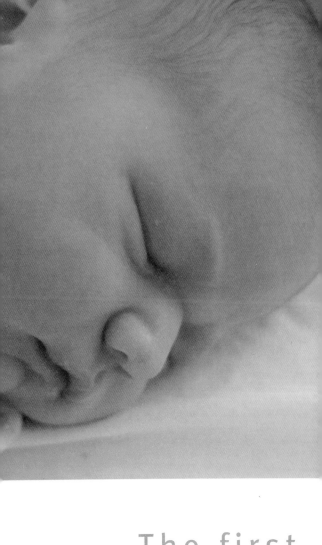

The first
baby

The most beautiful of jewels

On the day you were born . . . I made you grow like a plant of the field. You grew up and developed and became the most beautiful of jewels. Ezekiel 16: 5, 7

All babies are beautiful and, in the eyes of their parents, rightly viewed as the most beautiful babies that have ever been born. This is no less true of babies who may be given the term "disabled." 17 *They deserve extra-special love, and are often themselves even more loving than so-called "normal" babies. For God has made us in his image and loves us whatever we are.*

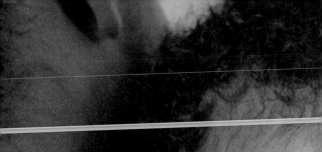

As a father has compassion on his children

so the LORD has compassion on those who

fear him; for he knows how we are formed,

he remembers that we are dust.

Psalm 103: 13, 14

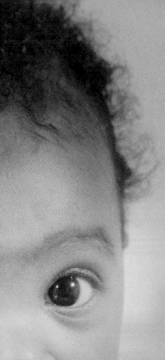

The best dad in the world

All fathers should long to be the best dads in the world. The idea children have of God is most often modeled on their moms and dads. If they are to believe and trust in a loving and compassionate heavenly Father, it is more likely to occur because they have seen such qualities in their own dad.

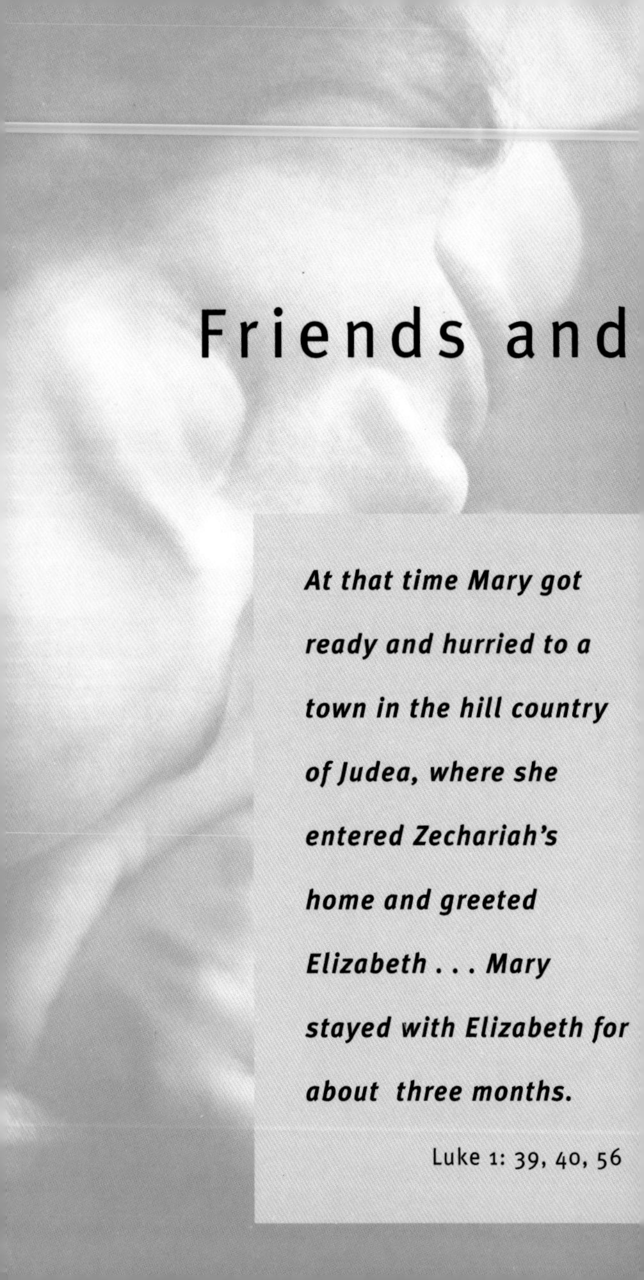

Friends and

At that time Mary got
ready and hurried to a
town in the hill country
of Judea, where she
entered Zechariah's
home and greeted
Elizabeth . . . Mary
stayed with Elizabeth for
about three months.

Luke 1: 39, 40, 56

family

It has been estimated that as many as 25 percent of new mothers suffer from postnatal depression, sometimes in the most acute form. Who is going to be around to help, when dad is out all day at work? A close friend or a trusted family relation can be an invaluable Godsend in the months both before and after the baby's birth.

A mother's love

As a mother comforts her child, so will I comfort you.   Isaiah 66: 13

From the baby's viewpoint, all he or she longs for is the love, security, and comfort of his or her parents. No wonder the Lord himself even likened his own love for us to that of a nursing mother.

. . . but we were gentle among you, like a mother caring for her little children.

1 Thessalonians 2: 7, 8

Little children

So what are the qualities that a new mother specially needs in the early months and years of caring for her new wonder-baby? The one mentioned in this verse is gentleness. For it is so easy to become angry and bad-tempered, especially when you are tired beyond belief, when your baby seems never to stop crying or will never go to sleep.

Peace
and
calm

"I will extend peace to her like a river . . . you will nurse and be carried on her arm and dandled on her knees." Isaiah 66: 12

Babies lap up love; it makes them grow. But this takes time. Parents are nurses, on permanent call. They need patience and calmness during the hours of playtime.

27

Part 2
Growing Up

28

Introduction Following the five negatives in the previous section, here are 10 positives as a guide for the growing family.

1   *If a child lives with encouragement, she learns to be self-confident.*

2   *If a child lives with tolerance, she learns to be patient.*

3   *If a child lives with praise, she learns to be appreciative.*

4   *If a child lives with acceptance, she learns to love.*

5   *If a child lives with approval, she learns to like herself.*

6   *If a child lives with recognition, she learns to have a goal.*

7   *If a child lives with fairness, she learns what justice is.*

8   *If a child lives with honesty, she learns what truth is.*

9   *If a child lives with sincerity, she learns to have faith in herself and those around her.*

10 *If a child lives with love, she learns that the world is a wonderful place to live in.*

God's love for us—the kind of love we long to show our own children—is described in terms of a loving father and a loving mother in the Old Testament. "I have loved you with an everlasting love; I have drawn you with loving-kindness." Jeremiah 31: 3. And "Can a mother forget the baby at her breast and have no compassion on the child she has borne? Though she may forget, I will not forget you!" Isaiah 49: 15.

An angel of the Lord appeared to Joseph in a dream. "Get up," he said, "take the child and his mother and escape to Egypt. Stay there until I tell you, for Herod is going to search for the child to kill him."

Matthew 2: 13

A fact of life is that adults can harm children. Jesus was in physical danger from the evil jealousy of Herod. Joseph and Mary took their child off to Egypt— well out of harm's way. There are countless physical, moral, and spiritual dangers today, particularly on the Internet. Parents have to protect their children by being constantly vigilant and unafraid to act for their safety.

Protect
your
children

Husbands, love your wives, just as Christ loved the church and gave himself up for her.

Ephesians 5: 25

Husbands have the highest possible example to follow if they are to love their wives in a godly and Christian way. They are to love as Jesus loved. Jesus' love was totally sacrificial and it led him to lay down his life. Husbands should give up their own lives in favor of their wives.

A word to husbands

Now Israel loved Joseph more than any of his other sons . . . and he made a richly ornamented robe for him. When his brothers saw that their father loved him more than any of them, they hated him. Genesis 37: 3, 4

34

Loving more

Every child is different and has different needs and qualities. Jealousy, envy, and strife between siblings can be avoided if each child is made to feel loved and important to their parents.

one

than

Raising children

Do not withhold discipline from a child; if you punish him with the rod, he will not die.

Proverbs 23: 13

"Spare the rod and spoil the child" is not so much to do with corporal punishment as with discipline in its wider sense. Raising children with just the right amount of loving discipline will vary from family to family. But God promises wisdom to those who ask (James 1: 5).

Lack of discipline

The rod of correction imparts wisdom, but a child left to himself disgraces his mother.

Proverbs 29: 15

We all want to be proud of our children. But there can be a real danger of parents imposing their own goals on their offspring. The trick is to be sure that we correct out of love. The correction must not break the bond of love.

For you know that

we dealt with each of

you as a father deals

with his own children,

encouraging, comforting

and urging you to live

lives worthy of God,

who calls you into his

kingdom and glory.

1 Thessalonians 2: 11, 12

Be an

Perhaps the most heart-warming thing any children can gain from their family is knowing that it is the place where they are valued and encouraged by

encourager

their parents. This will embrace every aspect of their life at home and at school, including their own Christian lives.

"Here is a boy with five small barley loaves
and two small fish, but how far will they go
among so many?" . . . Jesus then took the
loaves [and 5,000 people were fed].

John 6: 9, 11

Learning from children

This unnamed boy gladly shared his simple picnic. Andrew didn't laugh at the boy when he came up, and Jesus took this tiny, but generous, offering and increased it in order to feed 5,000 people. No child's gift of love should ever be treated lightly.

Part 3
Happy Families

44

Introduction Raising children is a serious business. But researchers have recently discovered that families that know how to laugh and play together are often healthier, happier, and closer. One of the best ways for families to stay connected with each other is to have lots of enjoyable time together as a group. One ingredient for such times is fun activities.

Christian families should be happy families. In itself, fun may be quite superficial, devoid of any real love, yet with lots of side-splitting 45 laughter. Times when a family enjoy being together can be greatly enhanced when everyone acknowledges that such moments of happiness are gifts from God. Paul writes to Timothy and says that people should "put their hope in God, who richly provides us with everything for our enjoyment." 1 Timothy 6: 17. God is the author of all good times. But we have to put our "hope in God" and acknowledge his goodness. All that is good comes from God. We are limited in our ability to create happiness.

Today many married couples have experienced years of heartache while trying to conceive and bear a child. Like families in the Old Testament, they know that barrenness is a dreadful sadness. Such deep sorrow is never to be skated over. Perhaps adoption is one solution. Many children testify to the great love that their adopted parents lavished on them.

The sadness

He settles the barren woman in her home as a happy mother of children. Praise the Lord. Psalm 113: 9

of no children

A word to fathers

*A parent who is out all day,
dealing with adults, can
easily forget the child's-eye
view. A distant response can
be crushing to a child's
spirit. Children need to be
affirmed by their parents.
Otherwise they may look
elsewhere for their love.*

Fathers, do not embitter your children,

or they will become discouraged.

Colossians 3: 21

Children, obey your parents
in the Lord, for this is right.
"Honor your father and
mother"—which is the
first commandment with a
promise—"that it may go
well with you and that you
may enjoy long life on
the earth." Ephesians 6: 1–3

Are children to obey their parents in everything? Here Paul states that obedience to parents is to be "in the Lord." So when there is a direct clash between a parent's wish and a clear command from God, a child is not meant to obey blindly his or her parents. The focus for parents is to be like God, so that children may see the good that they need to obey.

51

God first

Obedience

Children, obey your parents in everything,

for this pleases the Lord.   Colossians 3: 20

There is a need for children to obey their parents' direction, even if they disagree with them. An obedient child will learn self-control. But parents do not have the right to boss their children about and deny them love, care, and kindness.

"I want you to . . . go to my country and my own relatives and get a wife for my son Isaac."

Genesis 24: 3, 4

The long view

Children are a joy and responsibility for life. Parents are not supposed to stop caring for their children in their late teens or when they leave school. The elderly Abraham showed great concern for his son Isaac and longed for him to be happily married. To "be there" for one's children always keeps a family together.

*May the L*ORD *bless you from Zion all the days of your life; . . . and may you live to see your children's children.*

Psalm 128: 5, 6

Grandchildren

Grandparents can be a wonderful blessing in a family, and grandchildren can be a delight to them. With the older generation living longer these days, grandparents now often live to see their grandchildren grow up. Our society still tends to maintain the generation gap, but we do not have to follow this way of living.

57

But if a widow has children or grandchildren, these should learn first of all to put their religion into practice by caring for their own family and so repaying their parents and grandparents, for this is pleasing to God.   1 Timothy 5: 4

Caring for parents and grandparents

When children become adults, they are still children to their parents and grandchildren to their grandparents. Grandchildren and children owe a debt of care, love, and practical help to their grandparents and parents, and this repayment should be made willingly and with God's love.

Part 4
Jesus and Children

60

Introduction The Spartans were well known for their harsh treatment of children; it was common for them simply to discard unwanted babies. The Jews had greater respect for children than their Gentile neighbors, but even they often treated their children in an overbearing way. Hence the apostle Paul's remarks in Colossians 3: 21: "Fathers, do not embitter your children, or they will become discouraged."

So it is easy to understand the disciples' astonishment when Jesus took children in his arms and blessed them. Jesus was ushering in a new era when children would be valued, not as goods to be possessed or as livestock to be ordered about, but for their own sake and as heirs to the kingdom of heaven.

We may think that we live in a child-orientated Western society, but one of the biggest battles facing contemporary parents is to bring up their children in loving and godly ways, and not just follow the standards set by everyone around them.

Abandoned children

Everyone needs to be loved.
Orphaned and abandoned
children can feel that no one
in the whole world loves them.
But God has special love for the
fatherless. And while Jesus loves
all children, he has special love
for all abandoned children.

63

Though my father and mother forsake me,

the Lᴏʀᴅ will receive me.　　Psalm 27: 10

Jesus'

family life

Joseph and Mary took him to Jerusalem to present him to the Lord (as it is written in the Law of the Lord).   Luke 2: 22, 23

Jesus may have been born into a poor family, but he had the priceless privilege of being brought up by godly parents. We know that Mary obeyed God even when she had little understanding of what was happening to her. Joseph cared for Mary and the infant Jesus, and followed all the God-given directions he received.

Jesus as a child

Along with his family and friends, 12-year-old Jesus had made the tiring journey from Nazareth to Jerusalem for the Feast of the Passover. While Mary and Joseph set off for home, Jesus stayed in the temple. What amazed him was his parents' lack of understanding. Failure to understand one's children can happen in the best of families. Love and honesty put things right.

"Why were you searching for me?" he asked. "Didn't you know I had to be in my Father's house?"

Luke 2: 49

Then little children were brought to Jesus for him to place his hands on them and pray for them. But the disciples rebuked those who brought them.

Matthew 19: 13

"Don't bother your dad now." "Leave your mom alone. She's busy." It's all too easy to say such things. Jewish parents would bring their children to a great Rabbi to be blessed. But this was not a good time—or so the disciples thought. "You've got your priorities wrong," said Jesus. Blessing by parents or Christian leaders helps children to participate in God's life.

Jesus
blesses
children

Children and the kingdom of heaven

And he [Jesus] said: "I tell you the truth, unless you change and become like little children, you will never enter the kingdom of heaven. Therefore, whoever humbles himself like this child is the greatest in the kingdom of heaven."

Matthew 18: 3, 4

Parents who are at their wits' end coping with a demanding two-year-old may wonder exactly which aspect of a child's character Jesus was referring to when he said that people needed to become like little children to enter his kingdom. The humility shown in their trust and dependence is what Jesus highlights.

In these astonishing words Jesus is talking about the qualities of respect, love, and attention that every adult should pay to every child. Many adults dismiss children, patronize or ignore them, because children can't advance them on the rungs of any worldly ladder. God will never advance such people.

> *"Whoever welcomes one of these little children in my name welcomes me; and whoever welcomes me does not welcome me but the one who sent me."*
> Mark 9: 37

Don't sideline children

Harming children

"But if anyone causes one of these little ones who believe in me to sin, it would be better for him to have a large millstone hung around his neck and to be drowned in the depths of the sea." Matthew 18: 6

We can feel the passion and anger in these searing words. There are many ways of harming children: spiritually, emotionally, mentally, or physically. There are many ways of twisting their natures so that they become even a little suspicious, fearful, bitter, deceitful, less loving, or impaired. Woe betide those who are the cause, says Jesus.

Part 5
God's Family

Introduction God has great plans for every child who is born. To start with, it is God's ideal that every baby is born into two families.

First, there is the biological family. In the West this traditionally has meant the nuclear family of mom, dad, and the children. In the Old Testament it included a wide, extended family, embracing grandparents and great-grandparents, servants, resident foreigners, stateless persons, widows, and orphans. There is an African proverb that says, "It takes the whole village to educate a child." Family life is impoverished when it does not include the wider family, friends, or neighbors.

Second, there is God's family. God's plan is for children to grow up in the atmosphere of his love, which should be especially strong among those who love him and worship him week in, week out. Families should feel that they are being spiritually strengthened from the worship, fellowship, teaching, and sense of belonging that should characterize each local Christian church. As the Methodist evangelist John Wesley put it, "The Bible knows nothing of solitary religion."

Let us not give up meeting together, as some are in the habit of doing, but let us *encourage one another . . .*

Hebrews 10: 25

Belonging to

Children are the sons and daughters of their human parents and the sons and daughters of their heavenly Father. One provision that God has given us is the joy of being able to worship God in the company of fellow believers.

two families

The Christian community

But when our time was up, we left and continued on our way. All the disciples and their wives and children accompanied us out of the city, and there on the beach we knelt to pray.

Acts 21: 5

Children need to feel that they are part of God's family, and that the church is not just a club for adults. Children need no encouragement to go to church when they feel that they really belong to a group of their own age in the church fellowship.

Learning about

At that time Jesus said,
"I praise you, Father, Lord of
heaven and earth, because
you have hidden these
things from the wise and
learned, and revealed
them to little children."

Matthew 11: 25

Jesus taught that children have great spiritual understanding and perception. It's never too early to learn about Jesus' love: it's not a question of "When should we start to teach our kids about God?" In the prayers and love of their parents, children first know the reality of God and of his love, and that happens from their first breath.

God

Worshiping together

There was not a word of all

that Moses had commanded

that Joshua did not read

to the whole assembly of

Israel, including the women

and children, and the aliens

who lived among them.

Joshua 8: 35

A strong Christian family means worshiping together. The family of God is the church. Being part of a wider Christian grouping in worship binds us together in Christ the Lord. The Christian community should be composed of a whole range of people and should not be characterized by one type only, to the exclusion of others.

Unless the LORD builds the house, its builders labor in vain. Psalm 127: 1

86

It is often said that "The family that prays together stays together." The principle does hold true. If, as a family, Christian standards are understood and maintained, the household is more likely to succeed where this unity is built on the Lord, with each member playing his or her part.

Tell your children

Tell it to your children,

and let your children tell

it to their children, and

their children to the

next generation.   Joel 1: 3

*To their children, parents stand in the place of God.
In their early years what children learn about Jesus
and God should come mainly from their parents.
We are to "tell our children" about God's love so that
they may, in their turn, tell the good news to their
own children.*

Impress them [the Commandments] on your children. Talk about them when you sit at home and when you walk along the road, when you lie down and when you get up. Tie them as symbols on your hands and bind them on your foreheads. Write them on the doorframes of your houses and on your gates. Deuteronomy 6: 7–9

Practical help needs to be given to our children so that they can learn about God. We can read a Bible storybook or pray with them, or talk through Christian teaching. But in families, probably more than anywhere else, Christianity is "caught rather than taught." Rigid rules will least impress today's children.

Help your children

For your

children's sake

"I will give them singleness of heart and action, so that they will always fear me for their own good and the good of their children after them." Jeremiah 32: 39

The better people we are, the better parents we make. So if we attend to our own spiritual lives, we are doing about the most positive thing possible for our family. We know that people repeat patterns of behavior from their own parents. We thus have the opportunity, as no one else has, to influence our children for their own good.

Spiritual adoption

To Timothy, my dear son.

2 Timothy 1: 2

Not all Christians are called to have children of their own. Some are given the responsibility of fostering or adopting, or of caring for nieces or nephews, grandchildren, godchildren, or stepchildren. Many are given the high calling of nurturing children within the church. In Paul's letter to Timothy, we see Paul's deep love for his son in the Lord Jesus.

Mini Bible study Set out below are all the Bible verses quoted throughout this book. By looking up the individual verses and observing their context, a bird's-eye view of the Bible's teaching about children may be gained.

Genesis 24: 3, 4

Genesis 37: 3, 4

Deuteronomy 6: 7–9

Joshua 8: 35

Psalm 27: 10

Psalm 103: 13, 14

Psalm 113: 9

Psalm 127: 1

Psalm 127: 3

Psalm 127: 5

Psalm 128: 3

Psalm 128: 5, 6

Proverbs 22: 6

Proverbs 23: 13

Proverbs 29: 15

Isaiah 49: 15

Isaiah 66: 12

Isaiah 66: 13

Jeremiah 31: 3

Jeremiah 32: 39

Ezekiel 16: 5, 7

Joel 1: 3

Matthew 2: 13

Matthew 11: 25

Matthew 18: 3, 4

Matthew 18: 6

Matthew 19: 13

Mark 9: 37

Mark 10: 16

Luke 1: 39, 40, 56

Luke 2: 7

Luke 2: 22, 23

Luke 2: 49

John 6: 9, 11

Acts 21: 5

Ephesians 5: 25

Ephesians 6: 1–3

Colossians 3: 20

Colossians 3: 21

1 Thessalonians 2: 7, 8

1 Thessalonians 2: 11, 12

1 Timothy 5: 4

1 Timothy 6: 17

2 Timothy 1: 2

Hebrews 10: 25